Mexico

Mexico occupies the southern part of the North American continent and is populated mainly by people who are of mixed Indian and Spanish blood. It is a land of contrasts with arid deserts and tropical rain forests, high, snow-capped volcanoes and sun-drenched coastlines. This is a country linked between the past and future by ancient pyramids of extinct civilizations, colonial churches and cathedrals, and futuristic buildings of an avant-garde architecture.

The exploitation of large reserves of valuable minerals and oil has speeded the transition of Mexico from a predominantly agricultural economy to an industrial one.

Accelerated social development has gone hand in hand with this, helped along by the steady growth of tourism. These changes are welcomed by the vast majority of the Mexican population, who see this as Mexico's only way out of her current economic problems.

In *We live in Mexico*, a cross-section of the Mexican people, young and old, men and women, tell you what life in Mexico is like – life in the cities and life in the villages, life along the coast and life in the mountains.

The author, Carlos Somonte, is a professional photographer who lives in Mexico City.

UNITED STATES OF AMERICA

PACIFIC OCEAN

GULF OF MEXICO

•Tijuana

•Ensenada

Rio Bravo del Norte

Ojinaga •

•Chihuahua

Urique Canyon

•Topolobampo

Mazatlán•

Tampico•

Tequila •

•Guadalajara

Lake Pátzcuaro

Colima

•MEXICO CITY •Veracruz

Coatzacoalcos •

•Villahermosa

Palenque•

Paraiso Escondido •

Teotitlán Del Valle •Oaxaca

Acapulco•

Salina Cruz•

Guatemala

•Mé

Honduras

El Salva

we live in
MEXICO

Carlos Somonte

The Bookwright Press
New York · 1985

Living Here

We live in Argentina

We live in Australia

We live in Brazil

We live in Britain

We live in Canada

We live in the Caribbean

We live in China

We live in Denmark

We live in France

We live in Greece

We live in India

We live in Israel

We live in Italy

We live in Japan

We live in Kenya

We live in Mexico

We live in New Zealand

We live in Pakistan

We live in Spain

We live in Sweden

We live in the Asian U.S.S.R.

We live in the European U.S.S.R.

We live in West Germany

First published in the United States in 1985 by
The Bookwright Press, 387 Park Avenue South,
New York, NY 10016

First published in 1984 by
Wayland (Publishers) Ltd
49 Lansdowne Place, Hove
East Sussex BN3 1HF, England

© Copyright 1984 Wayland (Publishers) Ltd

ISBN: 01–531–03820–3

Library of Congress Catalog Card Number: 84–72048
Printed in Italy by G. Canale & C.S.p.A., Turin

Contents

"My father taught me to swim when I was two years old"

Luis Valderrama is 9 years old and lives in Paraiso Escondido, a small fishing village on the Pacific coast. He must cross a river and walk 3 km (2 miles) every day to get to school.

My father taught me to swim when I was two years old and I could fish by the time I was five. And now these two activities, along with exploring, are my favorite pastimes. My village, Paraiso Escondido, has water all round it. The Pacific Ocean laps onto the beach where the village is situated, and there's a wide river just inland a short way, with palm trees and mangroves on its banks. So you can see that there's plenty of opportunity for me to do what I like to do most.

My village is not large enough to have a school – only fifty families live here – so I have to travel every day, from Monday to Friday, to a nearby town for my classes. The school hours are from 8 a.m. to 2 p.m., and to get there on time I have to leave the village by 7 a.m. I then get in my *cayuco* – a small wooden boat which I propel with a wooden pole – and cross the river, before walking 3 km (2 miles) to the school.

Luis on his way to the elementary school he attends in a nearby town.

6

Luis fishing from his cayuco. *He also likes to swim in the river and explore its banks.*

My school is an elementary school. The children here are between the ages of six and twelve. Some towns also have nursery schools for younger children, but in many rural areas these don't exist. When I'm thirteen I'll be going on to secondary school where my education will last for three years. And if I do well in my exams, I can then decide whether I should go on to high school and then to a college or perhaps to a university, or leave the educational system altogether and become a fisherman like my father. If I go on to higher education, I wouldn't finish being a student until I was twenty-four!

At school I learn Spanish – Mexico's official language – mathematics, geography and history. But my favorite class is phys ed when we play football or basketball. I don't get much homework at the moment, perhaps only an hour or two to do each week, but in a year's time I expect this to increase.

When I'm on vacation, I like to get up early and explore the river in my *cayuco*. I always take with me a fishing line and some bait to catch catfish, and some small traps called *jaiberos* for catching crabs. And with my net I catch river shrimps which Mom always likes to put in her tasty broth. I also like to climb the trees along the river banks and jump from the branches into the water.

I like living here and am looking forward to the day very soon when I can join my father fishing in the open sea from his motor boat. Then I might be able to catch a very big fish, such as a shark or barracuda! But first I need to gain some weight and grow a bit taller, and until then I'll practice fishing for catfish and other fish in the river where it's safe.

"A bite from a rattlesnake can be fatal"

Eduardo Ramirez, 38, is the foreman of La Cienega, a ranch in the dry northern State of Sonora. He spends most of his day in the saddle, checking the fences and looking after more than 800 beef cattle that roam free on the ranch.

I was born in Sonora, a border state which has always been a cattle grazing area. And, for as long as I can remember, I have always wanted to work on a ranch riding horses and looking after the cattle. In fact, I learned to ride before I could walk, and was an expert with the *reata*, the Mexican lasso, soon after that! So it was natural for me to become a cowboy.

The *reata* is an essential part of my work. With it I can rope cattle and horses, and

Eduardo likes to entertain his children by doing tricks with his reata.

The reata *is an essential part of Eduardo's work. Here he is using it to catch a foal.*

remove fallen trees from the road. I even use the *reata* to do tricks, mainly to increase my skill in the use of it, but also to amuse my three children.

Chihuahua and Nuevo Leon, two other northern states, are also cattle raising areas, and together with Sonora, produce enough beef to satisfy home demands and still have some left over for export to the United States.

Not all the cattle in Mexico are raised on the dry pastures here in the north. Animal husbandry is flourishing in the rich grasslands of the plains of Vera Cruz, and now Mexico can boast of having over 30,000,000 head of cattle spread over the country as a whole. But compared with other forms of agriculture in Mexico, the raising of beef cattle is not very important. Despite only fifteen percent of the land's surface being suitable for cultivation, Mexico grows a great variety of important crops. Sugarcane, beans, corn, cotton, coffee, wheat, tomatoes, citrus fruits and tropical fruits are all grown, and these crops in general meet domestic demands and provide large surpluses for export.

Sonora, like most of the country in the north and west, is very hot, dry, and arid.

It is wettest in the summer months, but even then we don't get very much rain. This makes Sonora the ideal place for rattlesnakes, and when the temperature rises to 36°C (97°F) around 1 p.m., you can often see the snakes basking lazily on rocks. I only kill the snakes when they get too near the ranch buildings. A bite from a rattlesnake can be fatal, but thanks to snake serum, fatalities are now very rare.

La Cienega is spread over 200 hectares (500 acres). The cattle are allowed to roam anywhere on the ranch, grazing wherever there is pasture to be had. I start work soon after sunrise. Most of my day is spent in the saddle, checking the animals. I always take with me some wire, nails and a hammer to mend any broken fences.

I like to be back at the ranch house by 5 p.m. I really enjoy this time of day. The sun is not so fierce and I am able to relax with my family over a hot meal. Later, when it gets dark, I like to sit near the barn with my children and listen to the coyotes howling in the distance at the rising moon.

9

"Lake Pátzcuaro is the best place to live"

Juan Camilo is a Tarascan fisherman who lives on the shore of Lake Pátzcuaro in the State of Michoacán. The lake is famous for a delicate whitefish which is found only in the Michoacán lakes.

I was born in a town called Tzintzuntzan which, in the Tarascan language, means "place of hummingbirds." All the Indians around Lake Pátzcuaro prefer to speak Tarascan, myself included, even though we can also speak Spanish. Five hundred years ago, before the Spanish came to our country, the Tarascan Indians were a large and thriving community renowned for their bravery, their knowledge and practice of medicine, and their music, paintings and fine handcrafted objects. Today, we Tarascans are famous for the work of our artisans, our festivals which we celebrate in the traditional way, and for the

Juan and his wife check the fishing net regularly to keep it in good repair.

tasty whitefish which we catch in the Michoacán lakes of Zirahuen and Pátzcuaro.

Michoacán is one of the few states in Mexico that is blessed with green hills and mountains and with lakes. Most of Mexico suffers from an acute lack of water as there are few streams and lakes, especially in the north. There, apart from the highland regions of the Sierra Madre Occidental and Sierra Madre Oriental, most of the countryside is dominated by scrubland that is dry and arid, and irrigation is necessary to grow crops such as corn, wheat and beans. The beautiful, rolling countryside here in Michoacán makes it a popular place for tourists to visit, especially around where my wife and I live, right on the shore of Lake Pátzcuaro.

I make a living catching the fish that live in the lake. My wife sells the whitefish locally and it is a delicacy popular with the tourists. In a good night, I will catch 7 kg (15.5 lbs) of fish, not only the whitefish, but carp and trout as well. I fish on my own, but before I start, I have to cut a channel in the water plants that grow in the lake. I do this from my boat using a sharp hook attached to a long pole. I then drop my net into the channel, forming a sort of curtain, into which I hope the fish will swim. I do all this just before it gets dark, and early the next morning I pull up the net and, hopefully, the fish.

I have not been catching many whitefish recently. And now I hear that the Mexican Fish Department, concerned by the decrease in the number of fish in the lake, has opened a research station on the lake where they will grow fish in large tanks and then introduce them into the lake.

I do not know why the fish have become scarce. The number of fishermen on the lake and the way the fish are caught has changed very little even since I was a

After leaving the net overnight in the lake, Juan hauls in his catch.

child. I only hope that the fish farmers are successful in increasing the stock of whitefish here, as they are so important to the economy of the Tarascan Indians.

I have visited other places in Mexico, but for me Lake Pátzcuaro is the best place to live and to work.

"The passengers on my train are sightseers"

Valentin Lugo drives a train on the Chihuahua-Pacific line. The 920-km (572-mile) route crosses northern Mexico, from Ojinaga in the northeast to Topolobampo on the Pacific coast, and takes his train through mountains renowned for their beauty.

Traveling on the Chihuahua-Pacific line is a real adventure. It starts in Ojinaga, a town on the border with the U.S., in the State of Chihuahua. From Ojinaga I drive the train across Chihuahua's hot, semi-arid plains to the state capital itself, Chihuahua. This part of the journey is mainly through cattle-raising country, but after Chihuahua city, the train starts its climb into the forests of the Sierra Madre Occidental, a range of mountains which runs down Mexico parallel to the Pacific coast.

The mountain scenery which I see from my cab is quite breathtaking, particularly when the train passes through an area called the Tarahumaran Sierra, named after the Tarahumaran Indians who live there. This small part of Mexico has been designated an area of outstanding scenery, with deep canyons cut into the rocks by mountain torrents.

While in the mountains, the train constantly climbs and drops, through splendid scenery, twisting in all directions over thirty-nine bridges and through eighty-six tunnels, sometimes crossing above or below its own railroad tracks. At one point, the train reaches an altitude of nearly 2,438 meters (8,000 feet)!

All too soon, the train descends from the mountains to the low-lying land of the coast to meet the Gulf of California and the Pacific Ocean at the port of Topolobampo, in the State of Sinaloa. In all, the journey is 920 km (572 miles) and takes almost a day to complete.

I have been driving this train ever since the line opened in 1961. The route took nearly a century to plan and build, as it runs through some of the last great places of mountain wilderness in Mexico. The engineers who built the line moved an estimated 14.5 million cubic meters (19 million cubic yards) of earth!

Nearly all the passengers who travel on my train are sightseers. But there are other trains running on the line which carry such cargoes as cotton, timber, cattle, gold, silver, copper, zinc, and manganese. At

Valentin's train on its twisting route through the Sierra Madre.

Valentin admiring the mountain scenery from the cab of his train.

some points along the line, the trains can only travel at 10 kph (6 mph) because of the steepness of the grade.

Mexico has an extensive rail system, with over 32,000 km (19,900 miles) of track. The railroads were completely nationalized in 1970, and are now run by the National Mexican Railways. Most trains have a first- and second-class section and sleepers can be reserved for overnight journeys. Most Mexicans travel in the second-class section. American tourists, in particular, like to travel first class, which has pullman type seats and a restaurant car. Yes, Mexico has a lot to offer to the tourists, and what better way to see it than from the window of a train.

"It takes me about ten days to weave a carpet"

Celestino Bautista is 49 and a weaver in the artisan town of Teotitlán Del Valle, in the southern State of Oaxaca. He enjoys his work and is now passing on his skills to his son, José.

Only 6,000 people live in Teotitlán Del Valle, and almost all of us, including the children, make hand-woven textiles in the ancient Indian tradition. My father taught me to weave when I was eleven, and now my youngest son, José, is that age and I am teaching him the same skills. The methods of weaving that we use have been handed down like this, from parent to child, through the ages and have changed very little since before the Spanish Conquest over four hundred years ago.

The looms that we use are wooden and made locally. Some are expensive and cost up to 35,000 pesos (about $175). The looms are all manual – we use our hands and feet to operate them. And we use only wool to weave with, which we color using natural dyes. The dyes are made from fruits, vegetables and insects. For brown, we use a certain kind of nut which gives about seven different tonal changes from light beige to dark sepia. Pomegranates, tomatoes, watermelon and bougainvillea leaves all give different shades of pink and

The Bautistas working in the family workshop. The looms they use are all manually operated.

red. The cochineal insect gives a very vivid red. Lucerne and other plants produce different shades of green. It takes me a day to dye 10 kg (22 lbs) of wool and I have to do this twice a week to keep up with the demand – about 4 kg (9 lbs) of wool goes into just one carpet!

It takes me about ten days to weave a carpet in the ancient Indian design and color.

It will fetch about 10,000 pesos ($50). Sometimes I add my own design or pattern just for variety and for such a carpet I usually double the price. I sell my work in the town itself to both Mexican and American tourists. I do not like to haggle over prices as I think my work is cheap for the amount of time that has to be put in. The Americans, in particular, get upset that they can't bargain for a carpet or rug as they might do in a market, but they buy them anyway.

There are small artisan towns scattered all over Mexico, particularly in rural areas, producing a wide range of handicrafts for use in everyday life or simply for decorative purposes. Pottery is one of the oldest crafts and has the largest number of craftsmen. Silverwork also has a long tradition, not surprisingly, as Mexico is one of the world's leading silver producers. Cutlery, rings, jewelry and ornamental pieces are still made according to the ancient Indian ways. Many of the handicrafts are sold in Mexican markets such as the Libertad market in Guadalajara, or exported abroad to many countries, especially the U.S.A.

My work and the work of the other members of my family has been entered many times in handicraft exhibitions held in such cities as Guadalajara, Oaxaca and Guanajuato. We have even been awarded prizes and diplomas for our work.

Celestino and his son, José, stand proudly in front of a finished carpet.

"There is still much to be done"

Rosalba Nieto is an archaeologist. She is working on an ancient Mayan site in Palenque, in the State of Chiapas, and hopes that more can be done in the country as a whole to preserve Indian treasures for the benefit of the Mexican people.

I am working with twenty-nine other people to preserve the fine examples of Mayan temples found in Palenque, here in Chiapas State. The temples are being eroded by the wind and the tropical rains

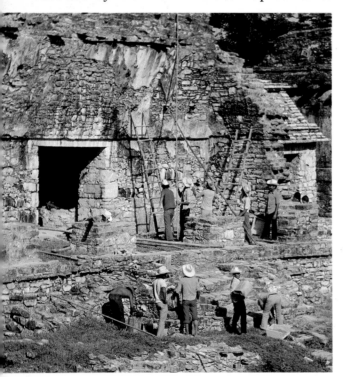

that fall in this area of Mexico. Part of the work is to remove the large accumulations of mineral deposits that have been left by rain water on the ceilings and walls of the temples over the centuries. We also re-build walls that have fallen down or look as if they are about to collapse.

It's delicate work and twenty-three of our party of thirty are local people who speak the Mayan dialect, with experience in rebuilding the temples of their remote ancestors. The other seven of the party work directly for the National Institute of Anthropology and History.

The Mayans were very advanced and at their peak, from about A.D. 300 to A.D. 900, inhabited a widespread territory covering Yucatan, southern Mexico and part of central America. The Mayans were accomplished in mathematics and astronomy, and from their Palenque observatory, carried out astral calculations to create a 365-day calendar. The Maya were also able to

A badly-eroded Mayan building which Rosalba is working on to preserve.

predict the eclipse of the sun with remarkable accuracy.

In this Mayan jungle capital are magnificent examples of bas-relief sculpture, and in other Mayan cities, such as Bonampak, there are frescoes which have been labelled masterpieces of the ancient world.

The Mayans weren't the only important Indian civilization of ancient Mexico. The Toltecs, a race of builders and warriors, founded their capital, Tula, in the eighth century. The Aztecs were the people of the last great Indian state. They were conquered by the Spaniards in the sixteenth century. Other Indian civilizations include the Olmecs, the Zapotecs, Mixtecs, Totonacs and the Chichimecs.

As a result of the rise and fall of these civilizations, Mexico has over 11,000

One of the majestic temples in the Mayan jungle capital of Palenque.

archaeological sites including temples, pyramids and palaces. Many of the treasures can be found in the National Museum of Anthropology and History near the center of Mexico City. I fear, however, that the National Institute which I work for, isn't getting enough money to exhibit all the artifacts that are being discovered even now on this site. I think it is important that today's Mexican people should have the opportunity to see firsthand the products of their distant Indian ancestors.

It's hard work being an archaeologist. It's very stimulating, though, and there is still much to be done.

"I especially enjoy the sense of flying"

Ignacio Sanchez, 34, is a professional high diver in Mexico's most popular tourist resort, Acapulco. He made his first professional dive at the age of 14, and has been a world high-dive champion no less than three times.

Tourism plays a major part in the economy of Mexico. With its beautiful beaches and warm waters, rich history and majestic pyramids, native markets, customs, festivals, and extraordinary landscape, it is only natural that people are attracted to this country. Up to 4 million people come to Mexico every year, most of them Americans, to sample what we can offer. And now there is a good national and international network of air services.

As you might expect, Mexico has a well-established road network. The Pan-American highway runs over 3,200 kilometers (2,000 miles) through Mexico, and Mexico is third only to the U.S. and Canada in the building of new roads. The railroad system is also being extended and there are

Ignacio and four of the La Quebrada *high divers pose for the camera.*

Ignacio feels that he is flying when he dives off the cliff.

major ports along the whole of Mexico's long coastline.

I live and work in Acapulco, Mexico's most popular holiday resort. Tourists are attracted to Acapulco, not only to enjoy the fine beaches and warm, blue waters of the Pacific Ocean, but also to see the famous *La Quebrada* high divers who dive 35 meters (115 feet) off the cliff into only 4 meters (13 feet) of water!

I started diving from only small heights at the age of fourteen, but by the time I was twenty I could dive 25 meters (82 feet) from the cliff. This was when I made my first professional dive. My brother showed me how to protect my face and stomach from the impact of the water while I was learning. As I gained experience, I gradually dived higher and higher off the cliff until I reached 35 meters (115 feet) and became accepted as a *La Quebrada* diver.

At present, there are thirty-eight *La Quebrada* divers, and to dive we have to climb up the cliff as there aren't any steps. When we reach the top, we pray to the Lady of Guadalupe asking for her protection when we dive. Fortunately, accidents are very rare – only those who are foolish enough to dive without constant practice are likely to crash into the rocks.

I don't know how long I will be a high diver. I'm now thirty-four and I'm not as fit as I used to be. One of the *La Quebrada* divers is fifty-nine, but I don't think I'll be diving at his age. I've done well in my diving career, winning three world high-diving championships in 1969, 1972 and 1973. It's hard, dangerous work being a professional high diver, but I like it. I especially enjoy the sense of flying that I experience while diving, so I don't think I'll retire just yet!

"I am at my stall seven days a week"

Agripina Montes runs a stall in Guadalajara's vast Libertad market. She sells a great variety of colorful native handicrafts from all over Mexico to Mexicans for use at home and to tourists as souvenirs.

I have had a stall at the Libertad market ever since the market opened twenty-two years ago, and I sell craftware made by artisans from all over Mexico. I have hand-painted pottery from Jalisco; carved wooden objects from Michoacán; traditional stone implements from Toluca; paintings from Guerrero and Morelos; and many other things besides.

There are scores of artisan villages in almost every state of Mexico, all producing handicrafts in the colorful Indian tradition. Some of the articles are famous worldwide – the artisan toys from Guanajuato, for example.

These toys were first made by the Aztecs hundreds of years ago. Unfortunately, there are now only a few families who are making them in the traditional way with the traditional materials of wood, pottery or metal leaf. And it is sad to think that one day very soon similar toys molded from plastic and vinyl will be seen on stalls like my own.

I like to think that I am hard-working and industrious. I am at my stall seven days a week, from 10 a.m. until 7 p.m. Sometimes my daughter, Liliana, helps me, especially during the school holidays. We form a good working team and I enjoy the company.

I have to pay to have my own stall at the market, but the rent is ridiculously small, 24 pesos (about 10¢) a day.

Not all the stalls in the market sell handicrafts. There is a large area of stalls selling fruits and vegetables – melons, tomatoes, strawberries, chilies and peppers, for example. There are also stalls that sell herbs and spices for cooking and for medicinal purposes. The medical profession has long been interested in peyote, which causes hallucinations, and other herbs and plants that are used to cure fevers and heal wounds.

December is the busiest month of the year at the market. This is when everyone is looking for Christmas presents to buy. In the summer I sell a lot of pottery jars and pitchers because the pottery helps to keep

During the school holidays, Liliana helps her mother on their handicraft stall.

the water cool and fresh. The tourists who come to my stall are amazed at the dazzling variety of colors, patterns and designs of the handicrafts I have on display. I never get bored selling my handicrafts. I even have some of them at home to admire and use. Mexican families have handcrafted objects in their homes, which is why I think there will always be market stalls like mine all over Mexico. So if ever you come to Mexico, please pay a visit to the famous Libertad market in the city of Guadalajara, and I will show you the jars, wooden instruments, painted works of art and other handcrafted work I have in my stall.

These are just a few of the stalls in Guadalajara's vast Libertad market.

"Flying is a common form of travel in Mexico"

Alvaro Guadarrama is a senior pilot with *Aeroméxico* Airlines. He has been with the company for 18 years and has wide experience flying DC-9s on national routes and jumbo jets on international routes.

There are over 160 airline companies in Mexico, including two of the major national airlines – *Mexicana de Aviación* and *Aeroméxico*, the airline I work for. My job as senior pilot for *Aeroméxico* takes me to airports located in every state in the Mexican Republic. In fact, there are over 1,100 airports and landing fields in Mexico and air services operate between all the major towns and cities. This is important in such a vast country as Mexico. For example, where it takes a day or more to travel by car from the capital, Mexico City, to Mérida in Yucatan, it takes only an hour and a half by plane. Airstrips are essential in mountain and forest country where there are no roads. In the tropical State of Chiapas, archaeologists are flown into remote areas in small planes where the only other access would have been by mule track.

The DC-9 aircraft I am flying at the moment is too large to land on one of those remote airstrips. It can carry over 100 passengers in comfort and safety and needs to

There are air services between all of Mexico's major towns and cities.

land at airports equipped to handle medium- or long-distance flights.

There are two ways to pilot an aircraft. The first is by sight; the other by relying on instrument readings. Mexico's climate and general weather conditions vary according to altitude and the time of the year. But for most of the time it is possible to see everything clearly as the sky is free

Alvaro and his crew stand in front of an Aeroméxico DC-9 aircraft.

of clouds, the visibility is good and it is calm. When it's like this I can fly the plane by sight. However, when I am flying through rainy season storms, which occur between July and September, or through dust storms when it's very dry, I have to fly the plane "blind" by relying on radio signals, and the instruments which tell me the position of the plane, its altitude, speed, and position.

Flying is a common form of travel in Mexico and is growing all the time. Passenger traffic is increasing by about 18 percent a year, while cargo increases by some 14 percent a year.

I get tremendous satisfaction from flying airplanes. I am in the air on an *Aeroméxico* flight for about twenty days every month and, luckily, in all the years I have been flying, I have never had an accident. I can't deny that sometimes I feel nervous, especially when the weather is bad. But even if I can't see a yard ahead of me, my instruments and the help from the control tower will enable me to land safely. My only wish is that I will continue to pilot my airplane safely and on time, right up until I retire – and that won't be for a few years yet!

"We don't have many visitors"

Kin is a Lacandon Indian. He and the Lacandon tribe are descendants of the Maya. Kin and his family take what they need from the jungles of Chiapas and sell handmade bows and arrows if they need money.

I was born in Naha, Ococingo, in the State of Chiapas. Kin means "sun" in the Mayan dialect, and this is the language I speak. The jungles where I live are full of life. Plants, animals and insects all thrive here, from the fertile ground to the tops of the highest trees. In the jungle, even a dry stick will grow leaves!

Everything I know about surviving in the jungle was taught to me by the elders of the tribe. From them I understand the language of the jungle: I can recognize every smell and sound, and I am able to see and

Kin, his wife, daughter and relatives rest in a sunny jungle clearing.

Some of the bows and arrows Kin hopes to sell to tourists.

walk through the jungle at night. I also know which creatures are harmless and which are dangerous. The fast and cautious deer, birds, and monkeys, screaming and arguing and doing acrobatics, amuse us. But there are also small, well-camouflaged poisonous snakes and other snakes over 8 meters (26 feet) in length, and as thick as my thigh. These snakes are so large that they can swallow an adult deer whole. Afterwards, the snakes look like hats! Poisonous plants and spiders as big as my hand also live in the jungle, and fierce jungle cats which are not afraid to attack cattle or children.

I am married and have a daughter. The jungle provides us with wood, clay and other materials for our home. It also provides us with fresh meat, plenty of fruit and water. There are even plants which heal wounds and cure fevers. We don't have many visitors to this inaccessible place. A city person just couldn't make it here.

I hunt animals with a bow and arrow. My bamboo arrows have vanes of parrot feathers, and the bow is made from a strong, flexible wood. I make my bows and arrows myself and I only kill and take from the jungle what my family needs.

It is not like this with outsiders, however. People come into the jungle to exploit its natural resources. There are oil rigs here and lumber camps, so our land is dug up and trees are felled, decreasing the size of the jungle. The Lacandones own the jungle and our chief organizes meetings to discuss land rights with the government and businesses. In some places the jungle has disappeared completely and been replaced by pasture land for huge cattle ranches.

I have traveled a lot in Mexico. I have been to Mexico City with my wife and daughter and thought that the people there were crazy. I did enjoy watching the television – we don't have it here in the jungle. I have also been to San Christobal Las Casas, in the State of Chiapas, with some of the Chamulas Indians.

If I want money, I sell spare Lacandon bows and arrows. I walk many hours through the jungle with my weapons until I get to a place visited by tourists – they usually like what I have to offer.

"I've worked with camels, crocodiles, rhinos and birds"

Clara Olvera Woodson, 27, works in Mexico City's dolphinarium. She trains the animals to perform tricks and in her spare time likes to read about Mexico City's fascinating past.

The dolphinarium here in Mexico City is next to an amusement park, so most of the people who come to watch the five dolphins perform are children. I put on three shows during the week and four over the weekend, each one lasting for about half an hour.

Dolphins are intelligent creatures and are easy to train to do tricks. And having studied animal behavior, I enjoy this part of my job the best. I always break up new tricks into steps that are increasingly difficult, and as the dolphin performs each one correctly, I blow a whistle and reward it with a fish. This way the dolphin will know that it has done what the trainer has wanted it to do and will do the trick again on command.

I haven't always worked with dolphins, however. My first experience in training

Clara is always training her dolphins to do new and spectacular tricks for the public.

Clara and two of her dolphins during a performance in Mexico City's dolphinarium.

an animal was with a rat, which had to be taught to do acrobatic tricks. Since then I've worked with camels, crocodiles, rhinos and birds. Once I even had to teach an elephant how to roller-skate! But of all the animals I have worked with, the dolphins are my favorite as they are quick to learn and have strong personalities.

In my spare time I like to read about the history of Mexico City. The Mexican capital now stands on the Aztec Empire's fabulous capital city of Tenochtitlán. It was a huge city with causeways and canals like Venice, temples and pyramids, markets and workshops. But in 1521, Hernándo Cortés and his army of Spanish soldiers and Indians hostile to the Aztecs, conquered the city and razed it to the ground. The defeat of the Aztecs marked the beginning of Spanish rule in Mexico and the exploration, colonization and exploitation of the country. A few years after the Conquest, the Spaniards built Mexico City on the ruins of Tenochtitlán.

The Spanish greatly influenced Mexico. Spanish is the official language of Mexico and is spoken by about 95 percent of the population. About 60 percent of all Mexicans are *Mestizos* – people who are part Spanish and part Indian; 30 percent are true Indians; and 10 per cent are pure-blood Spanish. The Spanish also brought with them the Roman Catholic faith, and now an overwhelming 96 percent of Mexico's 70 million population are Roman Catholics.

Archaeologists are still finding valuable remains of the Aztec city under modern Mexico City. Excavations for an underground rail system have unearthed exciting relics and the remains of buildings, many of which can be seen reconstructed in the city's museums. Even now, the remains of part of Tenochtitlán could be under the site where my dolphins perform. For me this is part of the magic of Mexico City. Everywhere I go I am reminded of Mexico's remote Aztec ancestors and their marvelous city.

"Movie makers come to this country to make Westerns"

Gabriel Figueroa is 75 and an award-winning cameraman. He has filmed nearly 200 movies and thinks that Mexicans make the best camera crews because they are enthusiastic, hard-working and very inventive.

Mexico has had a substantial movie-making industry for decades, and many American movie makers come to this country to make Westerns. The movie I am working on at the moment is about Mexico in the 1930s. It is called *Under the Volcano*, and is based on the novel of the same name by the British writer, Malcolm Lowry. John Huston is directing the movie and it stars Jacqueline Bisset, Albert Finney and Ignacio López Tarso from Mexico.

The movie makers who come to Mexico always prefer to use Mexican camera crews and technicians, and this movie is no exception. More than 100 people are employed in the making of *Under the Volcano*, many of them Mexican. I always think that Mexicans make the best staff because they are enthusiastic, hard working, and inventive. Many foreigners are surprised when they hear me say this, as they have an image of the typical Mexican dozing idly under his sombrero in the midday sun. This couldn't be farther from the truth. The average Mexican has little

time for siestas in the afternoons, he or she has too much work to do. It is true that some field workers will rest during the hottest hours of the day, but this is sensible when there are a number of long, hard-working hours ahead of them.

Television is very popular in Mexico and many bars and cafés have sets for their customers. There are seven television channels, three of which are government owned, and cable television from the U.S., too. The programs are mainly in Spanish, but some broadcasts are transmitted in English, French or Italian. Commercial radio stations abound in Mexico – I think there are nearly 800 in all, in addition to the government-owned stations which broadcast more cultural programs.

We are filming in Morelos, a state which is to the south of Mexico City. Morelos is very beautiful and its climate is spring-like all year long. This part of Mexico is dominated by the Sierra Madre, the mountain range which terminates here in the south of Mexico in a series of volcanic

The majestic, snow-capped peak of Popocatépetl can be seen from where Gabriel is filming.

Actors on the film set of Under the Volcano – *a film about Mexico in the 1930s.*

peaks from Colima in the west to Citlal-teptl in the east. Near where we are filming are the volcanoes Popocatépetl ("The Smoking Mountain") and Ixtaccíhuatl ("The Sleeping Woman"). An old Indian legend says that the volcanoes were once a Chichimeca prince and a Toltec princess who were forbidden to marry, and because of this the princess died of a broken heart. Now, when Popocatépetl's snow-capped peak rumbles, the Indians say it is the Chichimeca prince mourning for his dead sweetheart.

I love my work and I have worked on more than 200 movies since I started in the movie-making business many years ago. And, as long as my eyesight and health remain good, I will work for many more years to come.

"Oil is important to Mexico"

Javier Santos works for the state-owned Mexican Petrol Company (Pemex) on an oil rig in the State of Tabasco. He thinks the rig will strike oil located 6,000 meters (19,700 feet) underground.

Oil is important to Mexico. It provides energy for our industry and homes, and brings large amounts of international revenue into the country through exports. The petroleum industry in Mexico is run by just one organization – the Mexican Petrol Company (Pemex). It was formed in 1938 when the then President, Lazaro Cardenas, nationalized the oil industry. Since then, Pemex has made oil the principal extractive industry in Mexico.

The current daily production of crude oil is 2.75 million barrels and the daily production of natural gas is 4.3 million cubic feet. To get the oil out of the ground, to refine it, and process its by-products, Pemex has to employ more than 150,000 people.

I am now working in Pemex's Camp Aztlan, in the State of Tabasco, along with thirty other workers. We are drilling for oil, which the experts tell us should be

The oil rig at Pemex's Camp Aztlan in the State of Tabasco.

6,000 meters (19,700 feet) underground. The rig has now reached 2,500 meters (8,200 feet), so we have another 3,500 meters (11,500 feet) to go if we are to strike oil. My job on the rig is to test the soil samples taken at different depths. From the results geologists can tell what the likelihood of striking oil is, and so far the results have been very encouraging.

Camp Aztlan is about 90 km (56 miles) north of Villahermosa, the capital of Tabasco. Tabasco's climate is hot and humid, and jungle can still be found close to the border with Chiapas, another state with important oil reserves. Before the oil industry really developed, the whole of this area was covered by a large tropical forest, but now much of it has been cut down to make way for new industries made possible by the discovery of oil. And it is not only Tabasco's ecology that has been affected. The States of Chiapas, Campeche and Vera Cruz also have large industrial areas. Pemex, however, is now sensitive to the damage the oil industry can have on the environment, and is now supporting a move to preserve important natural areas and to decrease the possible damaging effects of pollution to a harmless level.

Oil refining has a special function in the supply of energy to keep Mexico working – 90 percent of the nation's energy comes from the burning of refined oil. And because of this, new refineries are being built, some near ports so that surplus oil can easily be exported.

Not all the Pemex oil rigs are on dry land. Some can be found in the shallow waters around the Gulf of Mexico. The families of the workers on the rigs are well looked after by Pemex. Houses are often provided, and medical assistance and other social benefits are supplied. What I hope is that Pemex continues to be successful and so help Mexico out of its economic problems.

Javier at work on the rig. He hopes that the rig will soon strike oil.

"Drinks made from cactus juice are very popular"

Don Pedro Ruiz lives in the town of Tequila, in the State of Jalisco. The town is famous for the potent spirit, tequila, which it makes. Don Pedro is responsible for more than 780,000 cactus plants, the liquid of which is distilled to produce the drink.

I bought my first mezcal azul plants seventeen years ago, and now I own more than 80,000 plants and take care of an additional 700,000 for some of the people living around Tequila. Mezcal azul is a type of cactus that thrives in the sandy soils and warm, dry climate found in these parts. And so important is the cactus to Tequila, that nearly all of the 28,000

Workers clear away the weeds from around Don Pedro's cactus plants.

Cactus plantations like Don Pedro's are common in dry, semi-arid areas.

inhabitants of the town depend upon it to provide employment.

The mezcal azul or *Agave Tequilana Weber*, to give its scientific name, has a liquid which, when fermented and then distilled, produces a strong spirit. We call this spirit tequila which, of course, bears the same name as the town in which it is produced. Tequila is a very popular drink and can be found in bars all over the world. With fifteen companies in the town involved in the production of tequila, you can see why the cactus plants are so important to the people who live around here.

A plant has to grow for eight to ten years before it reaches maturity and is ready for tapping. The cacti don't require a great deal of care and attention. The unwanted plants and weeds have to be cleared away from around the cacti at least once every three months, and I fertilize the soil every twelve months.

When the cacti have been growing for three years, I trim the points of the "leaves" to encourage their hearts to grow larger. The liquid extracted from their hearts when they reach maturity is distilled into tequila.

Drinks made from cactus juice are very popular all over Mexico. Cactus plantations are common, especially in dry, semi-arid areas. Many produce a mildly alcoholic beverage called pulque, which isn't distilled. Others distill a highly potent spirit, very similar to tequila, called mescal. And because fruit grows so abundantly in Mexico, freshly-squeezed juices can be bought from street stalls in towns and villages everywhere, and are much in demand. The squeezers, in very hot weather, are kept busy all day long. And, of course, we all drink fruit juice for breakfast.

At the moment I am responsible for sixty men working on the cactus plantations, clearing the ground around the plants. It's hot, backbreaking work and we have to watch out for poisonous snakes resting in the shadow of the plants. When we finish work at the end of the day, we relax and drink tequila in the traditional way — with salt and freshly-squeezed lemon juice.

"We have earned the name of Green Angels"

Filiberto Vargas, 51, is a car mechanic working for the Mexican Tourist Board. He travels up to 350 km (217 miles) every week, answering calls of help from tourists whose cars have broken down.

I have been a mechanic for thirty years, and have been working for the Mexican Tourist Board for the last ten years. At the moment I am based in the State of Vera Cruz, patrolling the state highway and answering calls of assistance received over my radio from motorists. I work five days a week for up to twelve hours at a

Filiberto patrols Vera Cruz's state highway in his radio-equipped "Green Angels" van.

stretch. There are dozens of car mechanics like me patrolling Mexico's highways, and we have earned the name of *Ángeles Verdes* (Green Angels) because of the distinctive green color of our vehicles.

My van is fitted with everything I need to repair the most common causes of breakdowns. Broken fan belts, dirty spark plugs, dead batteries or simply empty fuel tanks are all common. I am required to carry a fire extinguisher, but I prefer to put out a fire with Coca Cola as I think it works much better. I carry three large bottles of Coca Cola, and if there is a fire I simply shake a bottle vigorously to build up the pressure, and then direct the spray onto the fire using my thumb. It puts the flames out promptly!

I also carry a full first-aid kit in case of accidents, and all the information a tourist may want to know about where to visit and how to get there. I carry currency conversion tables, maps, and even a list of hotels that can be found in important towns and cities. I have to submit a report every fifteen days to the offices of the Mexican Tourist Board in Mexico City, giving details of the number of calls received and the type of assistance given. The data is then analyzed and filed for future reference. In fact, statistics show that every Green Angel is called upon to go to the assistance of about 100 motorists every month, and this figure is likely to rise.

The road network in Mexico is growing all the time and now it extends to well over 212,500 kilometers (132,000 miles). The number of vehicles on the roads is also increasing. There are well over 3,700,000 passenger cars in Mexico today, reflecting the fast-growing automobile industry we have in this country.

This is very good for the tourist industry. More and better roads and ease of mobility mean that people can travel where they want to, whether it is to see the majestic Toltec temple of Chichén Itzá in Yucatan, the pyramids of Teotihuacán near Mexico City, or simply visit a native handicraft market like the one held in Toluca every Friday.

I like the busy summer season the best as I enjoy helping people with their driving problems. I travel now with a partner, and between us we share the driving and make the repairs. We also give the van a thorough servicing once a month to make sure it's roadworthy and equipped to answer any call for assistance on Vera Cruz's highways.

Filiberto gives a visiting motorist some assistance on the roadside.

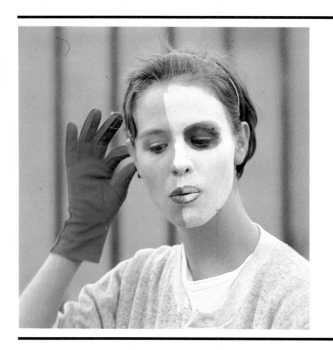

"Anyone can stop to watch me perform"

Jacinta Cara is a professional street performer. She has traveled all over Europe and Mexico giving performances and now supplements her income by modeling and by making ceramic pots and decorative ware.

When I was very young, I used to like dressing myself in strange costumes and performing in front of people. And I still enjoy it today! I haven't been to a school for actors, instead I have educated myself in the art of mime, pantomime and puppetry through performances on street corners, in subway stations, and in parks. I have performed in Veracruz, Oaxaca, Guadalajara, Guanajuato and Mexico City, and in Europe in such places as Covent Garden in London, England, and the Pompidou Center in Paris, France.

I really enjoy street acting. At the moment I am working with a friend, Diego Molar, and we call ourselves *Banqueta de Repente* (Sudden Sidewalk). The best days for our act are Saturdays and Sundays, but the money we earn isn't as much as we would get if we were working in a European city as acts like ours attract more attention over there. Because I don't earn enough money to live on from street performing alone, I model at art classes and also make ceramic objects. The modeling is not very interesting, but it pays for my ceramic materials and my acting make-up.

Color and art have always been important to me, and I admire the work of such Mexican painters as Diego Rivera and David Alfaro Siqueiros. Their murals at the National Palace and National University in Mexico City are universally

When she is not performing, Jacinta likes to make ceramic pots.

36

Jacinta and her friend, Diego, performing a mime for interested onlookers.

acclaimed for their flowing draftsmanship and color.

The work of mural painters can be seen everywhere in Mexico. Many painters are highly skilled and produce pictures of very high quality on the front of buildings and on walls. Many are commissioned by small businessmen who want to advertise their wares. You will even find the work of mural painters in the most unlikely places. A painter I knew was once asked to paint "No Spitting" and "Kissing Corner" on the inside of a bus!

The Indian sense of design and color can best be seen in traditional costumes worn at festivals. The costume worn at the Dance of the Quetzal is particularly famous. The quetzal is a crested bird that lives in the jungle regions to the south. It has brilliant green, red, and white plumage and the dancers imitate this in their magnificent headdress, which is like the huge open fan of a peacock.

When I am performing a mime or a pantomime, I am always struck by the different people who stop to watch me. It is not at all like a theater where you tend to get people of similar backgrounds and interests. With a street performance, I see people who are young and old, poor and rich, and of different interests. Anyone can stop to watch me perform, which is why I like doing it so much.

"The deer is an animal to love and respect"

Camilo Vecino lives in the Urique Canyon in the Tarahumaran Sierra, northern Mexico. He is one of about 50,000 Tarahumaran Indians who live in one of the last areas of true wilderness that still exist in Mexico.

The Tarahumaran Sierra, high up in the Sierra Madre Occidental, is a vast system of deep canyons cut into a high plateau by fast-flowing rivers and streams. The canyons are covered by forests and I have lived here all my life. My cabin, made out of logs and stone, is in the Urique Canyon. I live here with my wife and three children most of the year, but when the winter snow arrives, I take my family down where it is warmer and return only when the snow has retreated. We walk for long

The Tarahumaran Sierra is one of the last great places of wilderness left in Mexico.

periods, up to 6 hours at a stretch, along small trails that wind their way down the canyons to more temperate regions. About 150 people live in my canyon, but there are more than 50,000 Tarahumaran Indians spread across the region as a whole. Many live in caves in the canyons and on the high plateau.

Only a few Tarahumarans speak Spanish as we have our own language, Taracachita. I only speak Spanish when I am trying to sell the handicrafts I make from the wood of the Ponderosa tree, and the baskets from yucca leaves, to the few visitors that visit these parts. Like most Tarahumaran Indians, I have few possessions and live mostly off the land, growing the vegetables and fruits I need to feed my family. I also have eight goats and three chickens to give us milk and eggs.

When I was younger, I used to hunt deer in the way Tarahumarans are famous for, by running after them until they collapsed through fatigue. My parents and grandparents showed me how to run down a deer for hours, even days on end if necessary, by following the tracks and smells left by the animal on the ground. To us, the deer is an animal to love and respect. It has a special place in the hearts of Tarahumarans, along with the owl, squirrel and eagle, because we see them as being very wise.

We Tarahumarans have a system of laws which are different from the rest of Mexico. Each area has its own *gobernador*, an elected "judge" who serves the people without pay or privileges of any kind. *Gobernadors* serve for many years, settling disputes and conflicts that arise from time to time. Their judgements are always respected and followed without question.

While I am out walking, I like to sit at a high point and survey the countryside and watch the clouds moving across the sky. I love the mountains and canyons and the trees and animals that grow and live here. I know I could not live anywhere else.

Camilo loves to sit at a high point and survey the dramatic countryside.

"Mexico has a lot to offer sports enthusiasts"

Luis Bernal is a welder who plays baseball in his spare time. He lives in Coatzacoalcos, a town in the State of Vera Cruz. This year his team is entering Mexico's southeastern baseball championship.

I love baseball, I have been playing it for the last twenty years. The "king of sports," as we call it, is played all over Mexico, but it has a particularly strong following here in the states on the Gulf Coast, from Vera Cruz to Quintana Roo.

I play every weekend, with practice games at least twice during the week. The team I play for has been the local champion for the last two years, and now we are entering a major baseball league, the Southeastern Championship League, with top teams from Vera Cruz, Campeche, Tabasco, Yucatan, Chiapas, and Quintana Roo. With luck on our side and a good string of victories, we will be eligible to play in another competition against teams from Central America and Cuba.

Mexicans love to take part in sports. Soccer is very popular here, and is also undoubtedly one of the biggest spectator sports, so is boxing. Mexico has produced many world boxing champions, especially in the light-weight divisions.

Horsemanship and bullfighting go hand in hand in Mexico. The *charreada*, a form of rodeo, is a popular sporting event. In it,

Luis takes his son with him to baseball practice. Luis calls baseball the "king of sports."

During the week, Luis works as a welder for a construction company.

elite horsemen wearing richly embroidered costumes, topped by massive sombreros with specially-shaped brims, perform spectacular feats of riding as they lasso young bulls and wild horses. The *corrida* draws an enthusiastic crowd every Sunday at the world's largest bullring, the *Plaza de Toros México*, where leading matadors perform. However, in the country as a whole, bullfighting is somewhat less popular than in Spain.

Jai alai is reputedly the fastest ball game in the world. I have never played *jai alai*, but I have watched it and you need to have lightning reflexes and a good eye for the ball, just as you do for playing baseball. *Jai alai* is of Basque origin and is played in long, three-walled courts by two or four players. The players have wicker baskets called *cestas* strapped to their arms to catch the ball and shoot it out at high speed against the walls. Spectator galleries are usually provided where the top professionals play, and often there is betting which adds to the excitement of the yelling fans.

During week-days I work in the welding department in a construction factory. I am in charge of eight men, and together we repair bulldozers, steam shovels, trucks and other plant equipment and machinery. We also construct large tanks for the transportation of oil. This is a delicate job and we use metals of very high quality. The welds, in particular, must be checked thoroughly before the tank leaves the workshop. After five days working in the noisy factory, I look forward to playing baseball and the sweet sound of my bat against the leather ball.

"We need many more schools"

Rosa Valdepeñas is an elementary school teacher in a small, rural town in the State of Tlaxcala. She has been a teacher for five years and most of her pupils have farming backgrounds.

When I left high school at the age of nineteen, I went to a teacher training college in nearby Mexico City. After completing the course I returned to Tlaxcala to teach at

Rosa hopes to teach her class all through their elementary school life.

Lazaro Cardenas elementary school. The children at this school are between the ages of six and twelve, and I teach a class of eight-year-olds everything from Spanish to mathematics, although there are other teachers who take my class for music lessons and physical education.

Rosa and her class of eight-year-olds pose on the school's basketball court.

This being a rural area, most children here didn't go to nursery school – these schools for the very young are normally found only in the larger towns. After elementary school, the children can go on to secondary school, then high school, and from there to a technical school or even to a university if they pass all their exams.

The school is government run, and the education we give to the children is free and compulsory. The classes start at 8 a.m. and finish at 12:30 p.m., and there's one hour for lunch. Most of the children don't have meals in the school cafeteria, instead they bring their own lunch from home. There are also a couple of ten-minute breaks during the morning, and it is during this time that I mark the children's homework.

Tlaxcala is not a wealthy state, the ground is dry and not very fertile, and most of my pupils' parents are farmers with small plots of land and very low incomes. After school, many of my pupils spend the afternoon helping their parents farm the land!

Lazaro Cardenas elementary school is quite modern and it has a basketball court and a sports field. We need many more schools like this one in Mexico as the population is rapidly increasing. One estimate says there are 70 million people in Mexico and the rate of increase is 3.5 percent per annum. So there'll be millions more children to teach every year!

I like being a teacher very much and the responsibility it provides. I always try to communicate with the children, and never threaten them with punishment if they misbehave. I believe I can help the children much more in their school work and in their personal problems and doubts by talking, and this obviously works because I get visits after school and on weekends. They respect me because I respect them.

I get along with my class very well, and I hope to teach them straight through the rest of their primary school life.

43

"Mexican states have their own regional dishes"

Pedro Pascual, 51, runs the largest spice shop in Oaxaca City, perhaps in Mexico itself, selling more than 30 different types of chili peppers alone. His shop is in the city's well-known food market.

Chilies are added to many different Mexican dishes, providing a uniquely fiery flavor to the food. My shop specializes in this popular spice. I have more than thirty different types of chilies that my customers can choose from, and many other hot spices, too, which makes it the largest shop of its kind in Oaxaca City and, perhaps, in the whole country.

The shop is really a family business, as my brothers help me in its day-to-day running. It's in Oaxaca City's well-known food market, which is close to the city's bus terminal.

Corn and beans are traditionally the basic ingredients of the Mexican meal. Thousands of years ago, our Indian ancestors cultivated these crops, and they provide a cheap and nourishing food for millions of Mexicans even today.

Tortillas, a kind of pancake, are a staple food in this country and are made from corn and wheat flour. So popular are they that you will find a shop selling tortillas on almost every street corner! They used to be shaped by hand, but now the machine age has caught up with this traditional task and very few housewives make them. Tacos and tamales are other types of flour pancake and, as with tortillas, are garnished with a variety of chicken,

One of Pedro's brothers cleaning and preparing a basket of chili peppers.

grated cheese, onion, tomato sauce or chili sauce.

Many Mexican states have their own regional dishes and styles of cooking. Oaxaca and Puebla are famous for their "moles." A mole is a sauce made from more than thirty ingredients. One of the main ingredients is chocolate; another is chili. Chicken, turkey and other meat is cooked slowly in the mole, and nuts are sometimes added for extra flavor. In the northern beef cattle-raising states, which border the U.S., marinated strips of beef with a peppery tomato and garlic sauce is popular. And on the Gulf coast, seafood is popular and succulent dishes of shrimp, red snapper and bass are served with savory spices.

Until the discovery and colonization of Mexico, Europeans had never seen chili peppers, corn, beans, turkeys, tomatoes, avocados or peanuts. Cacao, a seed from which cocoa and chocolate is made, was first grown by Mexican Indians hundreds of years ago. And I know that Mexican flowers like dahlias, marigolds and poinsettias are common in gardens all over the world. Tequila is also synonymous with Mexico. This strongly alcoholic drink is distilled from the fermented juice of a cactus that grows in dry, arid areas. So you can see that Mexico has given the world many different things.

Pedro's customers can choose from more than thirty different types of chili peppers.

"Mexico imports more than she exports"

Horacio Guillen works for the Ensenada Port Commission, in the State of Baja California. He operates a huge rock-lifting machine and finds the large clouds of dust from the dry land irritating.

There are large ports up and down Mexico's long coastlines. Veracruz, Tampico and Coatzacoalcos are the chief ports on the Atlantic side of the country, and Guaymas, Mazatlán, Puerto Lázaro Cardenas, Acapulco, and Salina Cruz are the

Horacio's rock-lifter loads a huge truck with a 30 ton rock.

chief ports on the Pacific. I have been working on the construction of ports like these for ten years now.

I am responsible for a 70-ton rock lifter, the largest in Mexico, and it can lift rocks as heavy as 30 tons! The breakwater I am helping to build at the moment is part of an extension plan for the port of Ensenada on the Baja California coast. My job is to load

The Ensenada breakwater under construction. It will take more than a year to complete.

huge trucks with the heavy rocks, and these trucks transport them to the break-water for dumping in the sea.

I operate my machine in all weathers. During the summer, the temperature in this part of the world rises to as high as 40°C (104°F), and during the winter it can drop to below freezing at night. And when it is dry, there are huge clouds of red dust, thrown into the air when the rocks are blasted out of the ground by dynamite and by the large vehicles that are always coming and going. This dust irritates your eyes and gets into your mouth, and makes the work very unpleasant and uncomfortable.

The work I do is essential to the economy of Mexico. Through the ports Mexico exports her valuable resources and manufacturing products. Apart from agriculture, mining and petroleum are Mexico's principal industries. Mexico is one of the world's largest producers of silver, fluorite, mercury, cadmium, manganese and zinc, and altogether mining has shown a growth of about 20 percent in two years! But oil is Mexico's most valuable natural resource, and makes up about 31 percent of all Mexico's exports.

Coatzacoalcos, Tampico and Salina Cruz are important crude oil ports, the others I mentioned earlier export a variety of things such as machinery and transportation equipment (about 10 percent of total exports), coffee, tomatoes, cotton, shrimp and chemicals. Up to 70 percent of these goods go to the U.S., the rest to countries like Spain, Israel, Japan, West Germany and Brazil.

Unfortunately, although Mexico is self-sufficient in raw materials, she imports a large amount of machinery, motor vehicles and chemicals, the overwhelming majority of it from the U.S. And up to now, I believe that Mexico imports more than she exports.

The extension of the Ensenada Port breakwater is a three year job and we are about halfway through. I don't know where I'll be sent next with my machine. A few years ago I helped to construct Soto La Marina's breakwater in the State of Tamaulipas, on the east coast. I enjoy whatever project I'm working on, and always feel sad when the project is completed and I have to work in another part of the country.

"In pre-Hispanic Indian cultures, music was sacred"

Amelia Azar, 21, is a student of pre-Hispanic music. She has a huge collection of Indian musical instruments and thinks that it is important to find out more about pre-Hispanic music before it is forgotten.

I first became interested in pre-Hispanic music some five years ago, and ever since then I have been working closely with Mr Antonio Zepeda, an authority in this field.

Amelia, Antonia and Germán practice for a performance of pre-Hispanic music.

In pre-Hispanic Indian cultures, music was sacred and accompanied many important ceremonies. The sounds produced by such instruments as a large kind of marine shell, flutes, drums and *teponaztlis* (a hollow log played with wooden sticks), were all considered to be

something of the instruments they used from artifacts and from pictures, but very little about how the music was played and what it sounded like. After the Conquest, the Spanish music became popular and tended to overshadow or, at best, blend in with traditional Indian music. This is why I think the little knowledge of pre-Hispanic music that we have is very precious, and there should be more research done to find out more about it.

Dance and music often went together in pre-Hispanic times, just as they do in today's fiestas. A fiesta is a festival or celebration, often on a Saint's day, and so popular are fiestas in Mexico that more than 365 of them are observed in the course of the year — some of them are religious, others are secular; some are national, some are local. Nearly all are occasions for music, dancing, processions and fireworks, sometimes going on for a week or more!

Part of my work in resurrecting pre-Hispanic music is to give concerts. At the moment, the Mexican Secretary of Education is sponsoring a three-month concert tour covering most of Mexico with some stops in the U.S. I am accompanied in these concerts by Antonio Zepeda and Germán Herrera, giving two performances every day.

Through playing traditional instruments in the ancient way, I have come to understand how pre-Hispanic Indians imitated natural sounds such as bird song, the sound of the wind and rain, and the sea and insects. I am very excited at what we are discovering about pre-Hispanic music, and it is my ambition to make everyone here in Mexico more aware of this important part of our cultural heritage.

of divine origin and could be used to act on persons, situations and places. Some instruments were played to bless the birth of a child, others were played to give spiritual strength or to honor a death. Instruments were also used for more practical purposes, such as letting people know the time, sending signals or to give prior warning of the coming of rain.

Unfortunately, much of what was written by our Indian ancestors was destroyed during the Spanish Conquest. We know

"Once I captured an American murderer"

Enrique von Borstel is a customs officer in Tijuana on the Mexico-U.S. border. His job is particularly important in Tijuana as up to 1,000 cars a minute can pass through this border city from the United States!

My grandfather was German and came to Mexico when he was a young man. That, of course, was many years ago and I have Mexican citizenship. I was born in Mazatlán in the State of Sinaloa, and it was in this coastal town that I got my first job in a customs office as a cleaner, forty-six years ago. After passing some examinations to become a customs officer, I was sent south to patrol Mexico's southeastern border with Guatemala as a mounted policeman. I used to ride 45 km (28 miles) every day along jungle paths trying to stop the illegal smuggling of coffee and cocoa into Mexico. But I was soon posted to a customs office near Mexico's northern border and from there to Tijuana where I have been for the last twenty-three years.

Before I came to Tijuana, I was promoted to the position of major. I have had a lot of adventures. Once I captured an American murderer who was trying to hide one of his victims in Mexico. Another time I arrested a man who had one-and-a-half million dollars in cash in his

Tourists like to come to Tijuana to shop and to do some sightseeing.

possession, taken during a robbery carried out in the U.S. There are many, many other stories too numerous to mention. But you can see that being a customs officer can be very exciting.

This is especially so in Tijuana as over 30 million people pass through the town every year. Tijuana is the only Mexican border town whose highway allows up to 1,000 vehicles a minute to cross the border from America to Mexico! The people choose to come to Mexico for many reasons. Pleasure is perhaps the main one, and Baja California has many beautiful beaches and interesting places to visit.

The Mexican border authorities aren't the only ones with problems. The U.S. has to cope with many illegal comings and goings across its side of the border, too. The standard of living for many Mexicans, compared with Americans, is very low, and so there are always people trying to cross the border into the U.S. illegally, without the right travel arrangements or permission to work, in an attempt to get better-paid employment and a decent standard of living. But there are some unscrupulous Americans who will employ Mexicans for less pay than they are entitled to, because they know that they are there illegally, and so the Mexicans experience hardships that they hadn't expected. The respective authorities are finding it difficult to put a stop to illegal Mexican immigrants, as the border between Mexico and the U.S. is over 2,494 km (1,550 miles) in length, and there are hundreds of unpatrolled, unpopulated places where people can cross undetected.

I really enjoy my work. As you have heard, my career has been very varied and I've had lots of exciting experiences in the course of my duty. Baja California is very beautiful, you must try and come here sometime.

Cars lining up to cross the border. Baja California attracts many tourists to its beaches.

"I believe that Mexico is now overpopulated"

Fernando Hernandez, 26, is a marine biologist in charge of a project dedicated to the study and conservation of marine turtles. He thinks that Mexico will soon be looking to the sea to provide food for its large and expanding population.

Mexico has over 9,368 km (5,821 miles) of coastline facing seas which have some of the richest fishing zones in the world. The east coast faces the Gulf of Mexico and the Caribbean Sea. There, fishermen catch red snapper, snook, bass, kingfish, pompano, mullet and shrimp. The west coast faces the Pacific Ocean and from there come lobster, tuna, shrimp, and sardine.

The Mexican fishing industry has greatly expanded in recent years, growing from a catch of about 390,000 tons ten years ago, to a catch of about 800,000 tons today. Up to now, fish hasn't been consumed in large quantities in Mexico — vegetables such as corn and beans have been the basic ingredients of meals here for thousands of years. But I believe that Mexico is now over-populated and that in the near future will rely more and more on the sea for its food. The government is slowly becoming aware of this, and now money is being invested in projects researching both the effects of pollution and the study of marine life, particularly endangered species of fish and other marine animals.

My work as a marine biologist concentrates on the marine turtle. This animal is common in tropical waters the world over, and of the eight species that are known to exist, seven can be found in the waters off both the east and west coasts of Mexico.

Six months of my year are spent on the beaches of various states such as Sinaloa, Colima, Michoacán, Guerrero, Oaxaca and Tamaulipas, where the turtles come ashore to lay their eggs and then return to the sea. Part of my job is to tag a turtle while it is on the beach. The tag is fixed to the turtle's fin, and carries such data as the date and the country and beach of tagging. That way if the turtle is found again, perhaps by a marine biologist in another country, we can estimate how far the creature swims. I once received a tag taken from a turtle that had been caught off the French coast at Biarritz, the other side of the Atlantic Ocean!

I also protect the eggs from dogs,

Fernando at work, checking his records at a camp on one of Mexico's beaches.

coyotes, racoons and even pigs. Unfortunately, many people in Mexico, and in other Latin American countries, consider

Fernando making sure that these baby turtles reach the water safely.

turtle eggs as a delicacy and take them to sell. The Mexican government has outlawed this practice, but it still goes on despite efforts to prevent it.

I feel the world should be more conscious of the marine environment and do more to help conserve the turtle, and other endangered species like the whale, before they disappear altogether.

"You never know when you'll need to defend yourself"

Maria Ponce, 18, is a student at Mexico City's police academy. The training Maria receives is not easy, she does 16 hours a day, 6 days a week, but she thinks it is necessary because of the discipline it provides.

I've always wanted to be a police officer. Even as a young child I can remember dreaming of one day becoming a member of Mexico's police force. And now I am training to be just that, in Mexico City's police academy.

My day as a police student starts at 5 a.m. with a trumpet call, followed by a cold shower, the raising of the Mexican flag and an hour of physical exercise. At 7 a.m. I have breakfast, and by this time

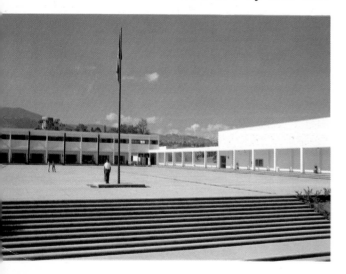

I'm feeling really hungry. The lectures start at 8 a.m., where we are told about general police duties such as making out traffic tickets, what to do at an accident and how to make out a report. After lectures, we have unarmed combat practice, shooting practice, or just plain jogging. Sometimes we are taught car repair skills. At 1 p.m. we have lunch, followed by more lectures and more physical activities until 8 p.m. when dinner is served. The call-for-silence trumpet is at 9 p.m. when it is time to sleep.

As you can imagine, the police training here at the academy is hard work and you need to be disciplined to do the same routine day after day, six days a week, during the four months of the course. I don't complain, however. I really enjoy it and it is necessary if I am going to make the grade as a police officer. I have two ambitions. One is to become a police motorcyclist.

Maria stands in the fine central square of Mexico City's police academy.

The other is to help end corruption in Mexico.

My favorite activity is martial arts, where I learn judo and karate. The skills of unarmed combat are essential in large cities like Mexico City, because you never know when you'll need to defend yourself against a violent person. Another part of the course I enjoy is directing the busy city traffic. This is practiced twice a week, sometimes during the rush hour, and is quite a challenge as there are over 2 million vehicles being driven in Mexico City every day!

Mexico City is very large. About 14 million people live here. There are wide roads and boulevards, thruway approaches, supermarkets selling food to suit almost any taste, and large, green spaces such as the Alameda Park and the Chapultepec Woods, which has 500-year-old trees.

The police academy in this fine city really looks after its students. It provides us with well-equipped medical facilities, uniforms, food and a monthly wage of 28,000 pesos ($140). My reports have been very good by all accounts, and I am looking forward to the day when I become a police officer.

Lectures are an important part of Maria's training to become a police officer.

"Pilgrims walk for many days to get here"

Leobardo Lopez is a street photographer in Mexico City. He works in the area of La Villa, where the shrine to the Virgin of Guadalupe can be found – the holiest shrine in Mexico.

There are fifty street photographers here in La Villa, Mexico City, and I'm one of them. We take pictures of the people who come to worship at the shrine of the Virgin of Guadalupe.

Leobardo and the large, colorful pictures which have religious scenes depicted on them.

There is a story associated with the building of the shrine. In 1531, it is said that the Virgin appeared to a young Indian boy named Juan Diego, and asked him to build a church in her memory. And to convince the priests of her wishes, Juan was to go to the hills of "El Tepayac" and pick all the roses he could find there (it was

These pilgrims have traveled by bicycle to La Villa to worship at the shrine of the Virgin.

during the dry, winter season when roses wouldn't normally be found on the hills). To his amazement, Juan found the most beautiful roses he had ever seen growing there, and picked the flowers and put them into his *ayate* – a large cotton shirt. When he returned to the town, Juan took the flowers out of his shirt while telling the priests his story. And when he had taken all the flowers from his shirt, everyone saw with surprise the image of the Virgin printed on Juan's shirt. The shrine to the Virgin of Guadalupe was built on the spot where the Virgin appeared to Juan, and today the Virgin of Guadalupe is the Patroness of the Republic.

In pre-Hispanic times, the Indians worshipped pagan gods – the rain god, Tlaloc, and the god of wisdom, Quetzalcóatl, for example. But soon after the Conquest, the Spanish started to convert the Indians to Christianity, and now over 96 percent of the population are Roman Catholics.

Thousands of pilgrims from all over Mexico come to the Virgin's shrine on her anniversary, December 12th. Many of the pilgrims walk for many days to get here, and so important is this day that it has become a national holiday. It's also the busiest time of the year for me, as I will take more than 100 photographs on December 12th alone, whereas I will take only about eighteen pictures on most other days of the year.

When I take a photograph, I stand the people against large, colorful pictures which have religious scenes depicted on them. I charge 250 pesos ($1.25) for each photograph. The photographs make a nice souvenir for the pilgrims who come here to worship.

I've been a street photographer for six years now, and I use a Polaroid camera, which gives a finished photograph in only a few seconds. That way I can work quite fast and my customers can see what they are getting right away.

If ever you visit Mexico City, be sure to come to La Villa and I will take a photograph of you for your album.

Facts

Capital city: Mexico City.

Official language: Spanish – spoken by about 95 percent of the population. In addition to Spanish, there are five basic groups of Indian languages spoken in Mexico – Náhuatl, Maya, Zapotec, Otomi, and Mixtec.

Currency: The main unit of currency is the peso, which equals 100 centavos. 200 pesos = $1.

Population: 67,405,700 (1980 estimate, excluding about 1.5 million adjustment for under-enumeration). Of this total, over 20 percent lived in the main cultural and industrial region in and around Mexico City, and about 46 percent were under 15. There are three large cities: Mexico City (with over 14 million inhabitants), Guadalajara and Monterrey (both with over 2 million inhabitants), and in recent years there has been a large movement of people from the countryside into the cities. Mexico has a rapid population growth of about 3 percent per annum.

Race: About 60 percent of all Mexicans are *Mestizos* (people of mixed Spanish/Indian blood), 30 percent are true Indian, and the rest of the people are of European (chiefly Spanish) origin.

Climate: The climate varies according to the altitude. In general, it is tropical with heavy rainfall in the south, temperate in the highland areas, and arid in the north and west.

Religion: Roman Catholic, but there is freedom of worship. More than 96 percent of Mexicans are Roman Catholic and only 2 percent are Protestant.

Government: Mexico is a representative federal republic divided into 31 states and 1 federal district (around the capital). Under the Constitution of 5th February, 1917, the legislative power is exercised by the Congress, which consists of a Senate of 64 members, elected for 6 years, and a Chamber of Deputies, at present numbering 213, elected for 3 years. Executive power is exercised by the President, who is chief of state and of the government. He is elected by direct popular vote for a term of 6 years and cannot be re-elected. Each state has its own constitution and is administered by a Governor, elected for 6 years, and an elected Chamber of Deputies.

Housing: The large and expanding population has caused a chronic housing shortage. The cities which have grown too fast have to cope with the influx of thousands of immigrants from the villages, who often end up in shanty slums. The government is encouraging new industrial zones where work and homes are being created, and work is being done to overcome insufficient water supplies and poor drainage in slum areas.

Education: Schooling is the responsibility of the state and is free, compulsory and secular at both elementary and secondary school levels. Elementary education lasts for 6 years, between the ages of 6 and 12. Secondary education lasts for 3 years, and opens the way to high schools and then to higher institutes giving technical and vocational training and to universities. There are numerous private schools and these must conform to government standards, and in large towns and cities there is optional pre-school education. The illiteracy rate was 29 percent in 1960, dropping to 12 percent in 1976, and is still falling.

Agriculture: Only 15 percent of Mexico's land surface is suitable for cultivation and more than 40 percent of the total active workforce is employed in agriculture. The principal agricultural crops are: corn, beans, rice, wheat, sugar cane, coffee, cotton, tomatoes, chilies and peppers, and many kinds of fruit, both temperate and tropical. Mexico is self-sufficient in the production of meat. Much of the farmland needs irrigation and about half the land worked is divided into small private properties, the remainder belonging to the state, which grants rights to peasant communities to exploit it.

Industry: The principal industries, apart from agriculture, are mining and petroleum, but in recent years there has been considerable expansion of both light and heavy industries, shifting the economy from an agricultural to an industrial economy. The mining industry has shown a growth of 20 percent in two years, and Mexico is the world's leading producer of silver and fluorite, celestine and graphite; the fourth leading producer of mercury; and the sixth leading producer of cadmium, manganese and zinc. The total proven pet-

Glossary

roleum reserves were 60 billion barrels in 1980, and current daily production is about 1,050,000 barrels. The steel industry has increased steadily in recent years and produced 6,949,000 tons of steel in 1979. Other important industries are: car production, cement, textiles (especially the production of artificial and synthetic fibers), paper, beer and consumer durables. Tourism is also important. Manufacturing industries and commercial institutions are mainly owned and managed by private enterprise, helped by public-sector financing.

The media: The Press of Mexico is in a flourishing condition. There is no truly national newspaper, though most of Mexico City's papers have provincial sales, and account for about half of the combined circulation of the country. In all, there are 178 daily and 21 weekly newspapers in the capital and other urban centers. The first printing press and the first regularly-issued newspaper in the New World were established in Mexico City by the Spaniards. There are seven TV channels, of which three are government owned. There is also cable TV from the U.S. The radio network includes 33 cultural radio stations, and 713 commercial radio stations.

Acknowledgments

The author and the publishers would like to thank *Aeroméxico* airlines and the Mexican Tourist Board for their help in producing this book. The cover photograph (left) was supplied by ZEFA.

arid Having little water.

artifacts Objects or works of art of archaeological interest.

artisan A skilled worker.

bas-relief Sculpture in which the forms are in low relief – they project only slightly from the background.

causeway A raised path or road crossing water or marshland.

cultivation The preparation of land for crops, and their subsequent planting, tending and harvesting.

delicacy Something that is considered choice to eat or having fine quality.

distill To purify a liquid by turning it first into a vapor by means of heat, and then back to a liquid by cooling.

ecology The study of plants, animals or people in relation to the environment.

fiesta A holiday or carnival, often on a saint's day.

frescoes Pictures which are painted upon walls covered with damp, freshly-laid plaster.

grade The amount of slope in a road or railroad.

husbandry Another word for farming.

mangrove A species of tree that grows on swampy shores or river banks in tropical countries.

marinated Soaked in a spiced liquid mixture of oil, wine, vinegar and herbs.

occidental The formal word for western.

pre-Hispanic A word used to mean the time before the influence or the coming of the Spanish.

serum A liquid which is used to immunize people or animals against a poison.

siesta A midday or afternoon nap.

sombrero A broad-brimmed hat.

Index